Midcoast Poetry Journal

Volume I   April 2025

Midcoast Poetry Journal
Publishing
2025

Cover Image
A Curious Encounter – wood block print
by **Alaina Zyhowski**

© 2025 Midcoast Poetry Journal Publishing

Midcoast Poetry Journal Publishing
is part of the Maine Public Benefit Corporation
Midcoast Poetry Calendar
MidcoastPoetryCalendar.com

sponsored by the twice-a-month
Poets' Corner groups who meet at
Rockport and Thomaston Public Libraries

All rights reserved. No part of this book may be reproduced or transmitted in any form or by any means, electronic or mechanical, including photocopying, recording or by any information storage and retrieval system, except in cases of short excerpts in reviews of this book, without permission in writing from the Publisher.

Print Edition

Midcoast Poetry Journal Publishing
15 North Street, Thomaston Maine 04861
MidcoastPoetryJournal.com

All rights reserved

Sarah Oktay's poem "Zen Geology" was previously published in "Sifting Light from the Darkness"

Sue Dow Thurston's poems originally published in "Reflections III-A Potpourri of Poems"

Katie Liberman's poem "Causeway Beach" was originally published in a column in the June 2024 issue of "Working Waterfront"

Published in the United States of America
Midcoast Poetry Journal 2025 -
[Poems Selections]

ISBN: 979-8-9929846-3-7

Midcoast Poetry Journal
Volume 1 April 2025

© 2025 Midcoast Poetry Journal Publishing

Dedication

For Jim Ostheimer (1932-2021) and George Chappell (1937-2019) who founded the first Midcoast Maine Poets' Corner at Rockport Public Library.

With gratitude and admiration for the staff at Rockport Public Library and Thomaston Public Library.

Cover Image by
Alaina Zyhowski

Readers
Megan Berman, Zachary Cole, Bill Eberle, Dagney Ernest, Len Germinara, and Mary Jane Martin

Layout and Design
Bill Eberle and Sarah Oktay

Editors
Bill Eberle and Len Germinara

Table of Contents

Megan Berman 3
Charles Brown 10
Eleanor Cade Busby 17
Steve Cartwright 25
Zachary Cole 30
Bill Eberle 39
Katherine Ferrier 46
Len Germinara 54
Eileen Hugo 62
Ann Leamon 66
Katie Liberman 73
Karyn Lie-Nielsen 77
Mary Jane Martin 82
Dave Morrison 87
Annette Naegel 92
Sarah Oktay 97
Jonathan Potter 104
Tamara Saltman 109
Karin Spitfire 113
Daphne Lehava Stern 122
Sue Dow Thurston 127
Harold Van Lonkhuyzen 132
Francesmary Vigeant 135
Dana Wildes 139
Alaina Zyhowski 147
Poets' Biographies 152

Megan Berman

Change

I am not her,
the willow wisp of a girl,
bending and bowing
rocked by every storm.
Not her,
the whittled-down wooden bird,
voiceless
hewn to fit a dumb mold.
A mute copy of the model in a magazine
smiling over a fresh-baked pile of nonsense.
I am not her,
the one who creeps gingerly over broken shadows of
yesterdays
who is careful to say the right thing, mousy and placid.
I wanted to be
I tried to be
What I am is much worse:
a bit of a peppermint hurricane word-soup
with a fistful of zazz and a hoard of desires.
Get your umbrella out, I'm on my way
to becoming

Perceptions

I could hear the sun's white-hot orb
boring its way through the thick mist this morning.
Preparing its yellow flame to scorch the deserted earth,
sear the sky the clean blue color of the fire's heart.
The cicada horde rub their delicate wings as one beast,
hearing nature's warning as a drumbeat,
as steps on the earth.
Be ready.
Days like these you can go to the sea,
or if the car leaves you behind, you can sit in the shade of
the porch drinking a tall glass of lemonade
(your sweat and the condensation on the glass becoming
one and the same).
Fanning yourself and talking of other hot days, chortling
over simple nothings in the heat.
Exhausted finally, impassionate and irritable.

Seeing the world as a flickering television set, bars of heat
rising in waves.
Mirages as glassy pools of water
popping in and out of the picture,
first here, then there.

In the late afternoon
a thousand gushing voices
come throttling down,
cutting through the buzzing heat.
A plop, tink, tap sound reiterates on the porch roof.
We stand on our shelves for a moment,
feeling the steam rise
smelling the warm earth
fresh-baked
its minerals the same as our own.

Megan Berman

A collective sigh
We could have died
But the sky brought us back
Another chance

I step out
the flowers peer up in bewilderment
I feel the rain on my forehead, eyelids, chin, outstretched arms
as I whirl and twirl like a child or an ancient giving thanks to the rain gods
a wild, joyous laugh from somewhere

Dawns

After crickets have done rehearsing night's interminable blackness, before the confounding traffic and brazen light of day

time slows

moments stretch

stillness presides.

All nature breathes in unison.

Dew rocks in rhythm with the flower petals and blades of grass as they
inhale,
exhale.

A drop rolls down a leaf and hangs, suspended.

Hyacinths exude their warmth, a veil of honeyed mist fragrant with night's lingering heaviness.

The pale-faced guardian of the night grows softer, kinder, as the sky brightens,
shifting to a deep-glowing blue.

Pink-pawed mouse and beady-eyed fairy
glistening spider and shiftless wolf
knit together in silence

waiting

watching

transfixed by the sacred wonder of each dawn's possibilities.

A cool breeze rustles through the birch leaves murmuring morning's silvery salutations.

There is still time to rest before the jays begin their daily song.

Morning

Over a cup of coffee

I mold my colors.

Then, I rinse the deep-rooted potatoes out of my bones,

pin on my stripes,

comb my features back,

paint my tights,

conjure a convivial, mischievous sprite,

then I stand tall and fit on my pluck

before stepping out the door.

The Things in my Cellar

A dank, musty sort of hovel
where water collects in stagnant pools, smelling of age
and white luminous strings from the silver spider's trapeze
make long, swooping drapes from windowsill, to chair, to stacks of boxes
and the occasional filtered light from the sooty old window
illuminates all I've left behind in the wake of my cacophonous life.

The world I was too frenzied for
now desirable, in peaceful repose.
I should have kept what I stopped caring for to remember
what matters.

I give this moment to you:
the once daily, precious belongings I shrugged aside and
never gave a second effort, second thought to.
If only I had been different, had more fortitude or foresight
you might have been loved.

Charles Brown

The Bookmark

I was reading a book on the bench beneath
our pear tree in the first sunlight of summer
when I realized the wind had blown

my bookmark away. It had to be the wind,
there was no one else there except
a couple of bees in the catmint and a mother

robin on her nest. It was a favorite bookmark,
a rectangular slice of an abstract painting
with the artist's name on the back—a name

I forget. I hate losing things so I got up
to look for it and just then that joker
of a breeze blew the covers shut. The story

was so full of twists I knew right then
it would take all morning to make my way
back to the page I was reading so I

chose instead to follow the trail
of the bookmark. Probably the wind
had carried it beyond the white blossoms

of the rhododendrons and through
the leaning fence into the gently lit woods
that border the yard in back. Secretly

I hoped it would lead me to something
in touch with the soft fracture of the day,
an old well, maybe, thirsty for company

or, more improbably, the unknown canvas,
lying under some brambles, needing only
my bookmark to mend its broken geometry.

Pangaea

Is it helpful to ask if animus and bigotry
escaped when Pangaea, the continent that
once floated near the bottom of time with all

the unlearned benevolence of rock, folded
and then broke like a porcelain bowl dropped
by a startled child, its jagged shards forever

skidding out from the event across a floor
of molten minerals as seething as hate?
The child in us wants to glue the tectonic plate

back together with the lost epoxy of oneness,
sees how the seven pieces of this jigsaw
puzzle of an earth used to fit as snuggly as

a river in a valley or an unborn infant
in its womb. But beneath the crust a force as
divisive as a rib spreader carries each away

from its distant self in a wrenching story of
friction and fault. And even if arms were long
enough to reach across the sea, the strength

it takes to counter continental drift lies mostly
in the heart whose walled-off chambers often
have been known to war among themselves.

The Leaf in the Road

I was bearing down on that little
brown leaf scurrying across the road
like a frightened mouse with a stem

for a tail knowing our paths
were going to cross and hoping
it would follow the line

of the tail pipe in the safe zone
between the tires and emerge
in my mirror every bit as alive

as a dead leaf can be, just
rocking a little in the crosscurrents
like a teacup on a table

that someone bumps into
by accident. I knew
it was just a November leaf

blowing across the road
in the cold sunlight with
no needs and no adrenaline

pumping through a tiny heart.
Yet mine was a piston pounding
in the cylinder of my chest

as my imagination sped away
before the leaf I had endowed
with life had time to die again.

Gusher

Who would care about sunrays streaming
through the windows of the co-op except
someone filling a plastic container

with olive oil in the bulk produce aisle,
watching the light infuse the rising tide
of green-gold oil flowing from the spigot

almost as slowly as the sap once rose
in the tree in California where the label
says it's from. No wonder it dazzles given

that olives are little more than drops
of sunshine in a semi-solid state
that just now are reliving their story

right in the middle of my container
as a slow-motion swirl, a strange funnel
of bright bubbles, gathers itself upward

and I can see the olive tree emerging,
first the trunk and then the branches and
pale green leaves unfolding like a strand

of DNA. It's good the co-op doesn't charge
for reverie, but someone might have told me
my cup was running over—still, I closed

the tap just before it did and capped
as best I could this shimmering gusher
of imagination with the thin, plastic lid.

Solar Odyssey

I doubt this idea will fly: levitating
solar panels that rise off your roof
when night comes and hover

in place as the earth takes you
for a spin through the dark - panels
that never lose sight of the sun

but stay tied to the grid
of your needs by satellites
stringing wire in the sky. Then

when dawn brings your house
full circle the panels descend
and roost again like birds on a nest.

At heart, it seems, solar panels
are homebodies so there is
something epic about the odyssey

of those Jimmy Carter installed
on the White House. They served
for years as faithfully as the Marines

out front until the next president
put them in storage - cut off
from the light and all but forgotten

except in Maine by a tiny college
called Unity that bought them
for peanuts, bused them to campus

and gave them another chance
at life, this time over the dining hall,
assigning them the humble work

of heating water for the kitchen.
Today those panels are icons, even
the one that floated off to a museum

in China. They may be unplugged
but they are still with us, survivors
of the first battles to cap the oil wells

that to this day are pumping blindly
in the dark while solar power travels
in broad daylight, looking for a home.

Eleanor Cade Busby

Moonlight Dancing

At least once in life
dance
on a deserted beach in lighthouse beams
with someone who sings
and holds you in their arms,
while the world stops on its axis.

Slip out of time,
into mystery,
to understand at last
the whispers of the stars
in their own language.

Live an eon
in that moment, spinning
spinning into eternity's love song.

When sunrise erases the memory of how you spoke with
stars,
bringing bare feet
back to the damp sand of misty dawn
—and mosquito bites remind
that you are only human—

Your soul will remember that night,
beneath the gibbous moon,
when you danced in the arms of magic,
and fleeting joy.

The Damariscotta River

Damariscotta wears her river like a ribbon in a young girl's hair.
Some days she meanders—brightly blue, sparkling,
shining as she passes the shore,
reflecting the fluffy clouds above.

Other days, shabby and untidy, she frays around the edges,
unable to control where she lands or stay tied neatly to her banks—
gray, lazy, almost feeble.

Days like today, she limps along,
a lackadaisical pat here and there at a passing boat,
listless, dragging small swells up only rarely,
sweltering in the heat, too damp even for a river to play.

But nights like tonight, when storms come in,
she'll show her true power—
lashing out across the seawall,
roaring into the flatlands, flooding the grounds,
and whipping the earth with gray sharp edges.

She unties small dories,
heaving them to skitter ashore,
while her water churns with electric ferocity.

If one lives near her long enough,
it just takes closed eyes and a deep breath
to sense what kind of tide will rise
Even then, she guards her secrets well.
She won't tip her hand—
not for the docks or the rocks or for you.

Eleanor Cade Busby

Her ribbons of saltwater
carry whispers of wildness and warning,
reminding you that it is she that chooses – who to hold,
and who to sweep back into the dark, endless pull of the sea.

The owl called back

I went to the woods
when the world was weeping,
to ask the forest for a blessing—
the scent of balsam,
and wind from the treetops that whispers peace.

The air carried a sharp tang of pine,
mingled with faint sweetness of cedar.
Moss beneath my boots
was soft, damp with rain's memory,
its earthy perfume rising in greeting.

The earth welcomed me.

Broken fir boughs lined the rough path,
ribbons of green along the snow.
Each step released their woodsy aroma.

Above, the sky shone bright,
bright clouds adrift in a blue so deep
the ocean beyond seemed to applaud.

Night crept in, its chill laced with smoke—
a scent of distant fires.

I must turn back toward the gnarled path,
toward the world
and its painful birthing again.

Then, a flutter overhead—
a wingspan, brown and white and gloriously wide.
A call: *Who...who...*

And, not knowing the answer,
I echoed softly: *Who,*
as my father taught me,
a greeting, a thank you.

He called back again, questioning.
I stopped to answer—
for that is only polite when your host is an owl.

We spoke, back and forth,
sharing woods, stories, wild sea crashing,
the incense of pine and twig,
and the eternal question: *Who?*

That dusk, my heart was hurting,
the world waiting—
but the owl called me back.

After the Storm

Oh, in summer, she lures you—
with silken caresses, cool at best, sometimes icy.
Her salty kisses reach every crevice,
even the hidden places.

She sings, undulates around you,
a siren of magnitude incomprehensible,
her breath scented with a menagerie:
shell, sea, kelp,
pine, or the remnants of flowers long decayed.
Clean—so clean— yet, for just a second,
that whiff of death.

She knows you will forgive her tantrums.
Her clutch on your soul runs deep, everlasting.
You are addicted to her—
her dark moods, her wild tumults,
her smooth-as-glass expanse,
perfect blue beneath the sun's golden glory.

In her arms, you float.
In her love, you drown.
Oh, how you breathe her in, every sigh.

And when she throws rocks at you,
lashes you with fury,
slaps your face with icy fingers,
she knows—
she knows.

All she must do is wait and retreat,
simply be her majestic self.

And you will draw your breath in wonder,
still loving her.

And while you may not forget,
you forgive.
You forgive.
You come back for more—
for her saltwater runs in your veins.

Charlie's Hands

Charlie said his hands
were old man's hands,
but I saw fingers caress piano keys,
dancing music from ivory and wood.

Charlie's hands are the hands
of a lover, soothing a weary brow.

Charlie said his hands
were old man's hands.
He saw tendons and brown spots,
but I saw moments of joy
in the sun and the rain,
strength to carry on and to carry others.

Charlie said his hands
were old man's hands,
but I saw a victory written there,
one we never would have dreamed
in the long ago.

Charlie's hands hold other hands—
in love and in sorrow.

Charlie's hands coax laughter and delight
from tired minds and hearts,
music healing wounds
before the door closes.
Charlie said his hands were
old man's hands.

How I love that Charlie can say that still,
his touch on the keys soothing, loving, serenading—
and the world is blessed by Charlie's hands.

Steve Cartwright

Joel

He ran he danced
Planted and harvested
Loved his little sister
And all living beings

Black clouds came early
Blocking sunlight and joy
"I hate myself even more
Than I love you" he wrote

No hope no help no cure
Sinking in a dark sea
with a deadly undertow

One summer day
One gun one bullet
Everything ends

He ran he danced
He planted and harvested
Loved his little sister
And all living beings

Epitaph

I was writing in bright morning light
I call my editor who said what's it matter?
We're at war
September 11, 2001, the twin towers fall
Along with illusions, the greatest no more
Terrorists, we scream; to name them, to blame
Those who used our planes against us
They outsmarted an arrogant nation
That plows billions into war
Only to reap
A harvest of hate

Tighten security
Put a noose around freedom
Some say we had it coming
But when will we ask why?
Answers lie in the shadows

Headlines

Today I catch the news
The world is
Coming to an end
Not a hoax, not fake news
Should've slept in
But the shivery truth is
Climate change is coming to a place near you
It will soon howl at your door
It takes us by storm, flood, hurricane, drought
We heed it not

We still breathe, eat and drink
We drive cars, run leaf blowers
Because the bigger truth is too big
Too dismal, too threatening, so
We blow it away like so many leaves
And drive on

The news is not good
The air, the land and sea
Are sick
I drink muddy coffee while
I ponder coming disaster
and ask myself
What to do

With the rest of the day
With the rest of my life

Blue Heron

Heron, poised in shallows
holding still
holding grief
as if this bird itself
was the one I miss

Great blue heron returns
morning after morning,
mysterious, alone
we watch each other
my vision blurs

Heron steps lightly
on watery stones
and finally, takes flight
its big slow wings
the beat of a broken heart

Catterel vs Doggerel

Easier to be down than up
Easier to drown like a rat
And that's why you need a cat

When things look grim and drear
When sadness weighs you down
It's nice to have a kitty near

Dogs you know are often needy
Cats are happy on their own
True, at least, of cats I've known

Cats are clever
Suffer? Never

Einstein, Twain admired cats
wrote loving tributes to
These aristocrats

Mark Twain once said, "I simply can't resist a cat, particularly a purring one. They are the cleanest, cunningest, and most intelligent things I know, outside of the girl you love, of course."- said Twain, "When a man loves cats, I am his friend and comrade, without further introduction."

Zachary Cole

Six Tubs of Broken Glass

Every Wednesday morning I'm greeted by
six rectangular plastic tubs
filled with broken glass

I grab one by the handle and pour
the glass into an empty fifty-gallon drum
with a faded BANANA CREAM label

when the drum is full I hook a dolly
onto the lip and wheel the cumbersome
barrel of glass through the store
avoiding displays and customers

the grocery manager nods when I reach the
backroom and unlocks the loading bay doors
wispy snowflakes flutter into the room
dusting expired bottles of Mountain Dew

the loading dock is dotted with blue ice melt
I slide on a bare patch of cement and grab a
petrified palette to steady myself
I unlatch the drum and it leaps off the dolly
like an anxious kid running outside to play in the snow

there's only one empty barrel for me to take
someone moved it with a forklift and now
the barrel's alarmingly thin in the middle like Vampira

Zachary Cole

I spend a quiet moment listening
to unseen snowplows scraping the parking lot
snowflakes swirl into the
BANANA CREAM barrel

fifty gallons of broken glass
topped with a layer of whipped cream

Silent Night

All is quiet at the Green
all is calm

Walk past the Paul Bunyan flagpole
the cemetery where hanged men rest

Guess your way onto the gravel path
listen to the rocks crunch under your boots

Your guiding light a ten foot
Christmas tree guarding the gazebo

When you reach the steps warm orange light
spills onto your gloves, turns the world amber

Spend just a few silent moments standing before
this hearth without a fire

Witnessing a Murder

When I was twelve my friend
invited me over so we could
witness a murder

Leaning against his windowsill we watched
in hunched silence as a twitchy man with
dirty blonde hair marched around the
house across the street, screaming

He stormed into the neighbor's home, gun in hand
a moment later we heard a loud pop
and a young woman screaming

One long moment of silence, then the killer
stepped back outside, all smiles
asked for a Poland Spring and
sat down on the curb

Soon the young man he had murdered
joined him on the sidewalk
his left eye an empty red socket

"That was so freaking cool" my friend said
he was brave enough to head outside and
talk to the one eyed man
a young actor named Nick

I was too hesitant to cross the street
I said it was because I didn't want to
annoy the *In the Bedroom* crew

But in truth I was rattled by the unbridled
intensity of the dirty blonde man
in my head that incredible actor is not in Hollywood
or rehearsing lines on location in Hawaii
he's still roaming Grove Street in Rockland
gun in hand, looking for his next victim

humble

When I was seven the humble Farmer
traveled to my neighborhood in his
trademark white Model T
I was too shy to meet him
but all day I imagined climbing into
his classic car and joyriding
with one of my childhood idols

Twenty years later I'm walking past
Wasses Hot Dogs at dusk when that same
Model T grinds to a stop
The humble Farmer wants to know
where the nearest gun shop is

I feign ignorance
concerned that I'll become an accessory
to some crime after the fact

but agree to a dreamlike ride
in his ancient auto
we spew kerosene all over Thomaston
a town I hardly know
he raves about the TG where the
coffee's free and the conversation rich
and the Mall where trolleys used to pull in before
cars like his drove away the competition!

Zach you're going to love this place
when you move here in six years or so
and a few years after that
I'll be off to meet my Maker
you'll think back to this ride and wonder
How on Earth did that old man know
when *he was going to kick the bucket?*

He chuckles and floors the Model T
the future a winding valley up ahead
our backs to the sun
faces bathed in the light
of a new moon

Zachary Cole

Ship in a Bottle

I cut through the backyard of my childhood home
to reach Mrs. Johnson's house, yellow with burgundy trim
weeds have begun to investigate the cracks in her driveway
but that doesn't matter—she hasn't driven in years
her boat of a Chevrolet lies under a tarp in the garage

Her backyard is small, partially fenced by Mr. Wink
but you can still see the empty playground next door
I walk to her back porch and the door's open
she's turned away from me, carefully slicing bananas
so brown they've attracted fruit flies

I pass the icebox, her name for the refrigerator
and enter the parlor, her name for the living room
two wingback chairs guard a glass coffee table
the parlor is too quiet so I explore upstairs
her room is full of faded dresses sleeping in plastic bags

I use the bathroom, mostly to read her tattered book of puns
once I left the water running and the sink overflowed
so today I check, then double check the faucet before
heading back downstairs and am greeted by a glass bowl
gleaming on the coffee table—white popcorn mixed with M&Ms
baffling because Mrs. Johnson is still in the kitchen
I can hear her Pyrex loaf pan sliding onto the oven rack

Mrs. Johnson's gray shadow glides over photos of her dead husband
and I must accept with some sadness that I am in
a dream
Mrs. Johnson will never leave her kitchen and join me in the parlor
but I can explore other places I remember well
the quiet study where sailboats in impossible bottles

rode the lacquered waves of her windowsill
I typed my first story there, a Superman adventure
on a blue electric typewriter that came with its own suitcase
I can remember when she fell and broke her hip on the lawn
or jump ahead to the last time I saw her, at a nursing home
on her 97th birthday

I wanted to tell her that she was my third grandmother
that her quiet home filled me with a deep calm
that I've been trying to recapture my entire adult life
but I realized that she didn't recognize me
so now those memories are mine and mine alone
I can dust them off, hold them up to the light
but I can never remove the ship from that impossible bottle
and hold it in my hand

Bill Eberle

being useful

I said I would keep on living
as long as I was useful

She asked
"Do you consider being a lap for a cat useful?"
and I said, "Of course."

and as I mulled that over
thinking of people and cats I've loved and love
I thought

"Perhaps as long as I can still love
a person or a cat
I can still be useful."

and later I thought

> "What can that love teach me
> about how to go about
> living from now
> until when
> I finally
> wear
> out?"

and the answer came back

> "Feel that love as much as possible
> in everything you think
> communicate
> create
> and
> do."

Maine

it's not that there's more kindness
it's not that easy

instead
there's
a little space of time
a pause
a slowing of the pace
that allows
recognition
and kindness
to happen

paddle board

my wife has a paddle board

on our ninth anniversary
she walks out on the water
until she's a small figure
near the horizon

exploring
moving cleanly across the surface

I can feel her joy and her serenity
from here in my beach chair

now she comes back
diagonally to the shallows
and sits watching the small crabs
beneath her

artist

these colors and textures
wild nature
brambles thorns

trees some already gone
leaning or
the largest
still standing tall

a stream
a torrent with a lot of rain
gentle now

on this middle May day
such a coming together
of different colors

scenes some might call ugly
piles of brush and branches
a rotting woodpile birthing mushrooms

but the artist sees differently
sees everything as one big canvas

and is mesmerized
by each brushstroke
each detail
captured
perfectly

Bill Eberle

in a trance
of noticing each place out there
and imagining the artist's process

until a bee
flies into the picture
buzzes around a nearby
empty chair
then around a tree
and then gone

struck then by the idea
that the canvas is a movie
instantly re-created each moment
in every direction
with motion and action
revealed as the frames
fly by

and the artist laughs
and is grateful for the artistry

of existence

equal

we might say
we live in a country that guarantees
"equal protection under the law"
but our history proves
otherwise

it's a losing battle
that must be continuously fought
uphill
against the implacable
ever present foes
ignorance
greed
prejudice
hate
and the seed of them all
fear

an impossible struggle
that must be endured
each generation
by all who can't not see

for the poor
for the broken
for the silent

basic healthcare not offered
healthy food and safe water
not available
fairness and justice
out of reach

Bill Eberle

the losing battle
must be fought again and again

one person
one family
one situation
at a time

to bring the truth a little bit closer
to our noble wishes
and the promise
of our original goal

"equal protection under the law"

Katherine Ferrier

Wayfinding

To begin, take a walk.
To find your way, follow anything.
Write down what you see:
zero, infinity, five
in other words,
nothing, everything, and how much can you hold.

When you can't see where you're going
eventually everything reads as instructions,
like the day you left for your new life in Maine,
stopping to get your packed car inspected.
How you waited outside for the work to be done
studying the poem on the peeling vinyl above the garage
shocks   exhaust   tires   brakes   alignment

Before Buckminster Fuller could make his map of the world
he had to make language big enough to hold it.
Dymaxion, for dynamic maximum tension
the word a portmanteau, a collection
of syllables, patchworked together.

If you want to make a map that fits a body,
that is, one that considers both depth and volume,
you need to cut it up along its meridians
otherwise known as seams.
When laid out flat, you won't recognize the shape.
You will doubt yourself and wonder
if there are pieces missing.
You will see the spaces where stitches,

also known as sutures, will be.
You will learn their names:
running stitch, back stitch, blanket, and ladder.

You will learn over and over the kind of patience
only knots can teach you.
You will come to trust the tangle as ally,
as guide, as portal, as atlas, as chart,
as the most accurate outline
of the poem itself.

Dreams of Flying

What if every question is a tether
connecting us to the ascending unknowable?
I spy with my little eye something so blue.
Something so far away as to appear near.

From the top of Federal Hill we calculate losses,
ponder the incline, wonder if we fell, would we tumble into traffic,
or would we remember how to stumble up
into the awkward flail that counts as flying?

Are you ready? is the soft question we long for,
though rarely are offered by the shock of what comes.
Everyone loves the sound of the wind as long as it's far away
It's the sudden gusts that topple us, tear the tops of our houses,
pull muttered curses from under our breath.

What do you see when you let yourself get close?
Below us, the Butterfly City opens her glistening wings.
You inch your small body too close to the edge,
and I reach for the hem of your green hoodie
ready to make your falling body into a kite.

What was your name when you were snow?
Every day I hold a cold letter in my mouth, ask the air
to deliver it, imagine the sky littered with white paper.
Syllables, alphabets, acrobats hover
in the already dissolving residue
of you, the other you, the one I said no to.

Katherine Ferrier

Can I make a plane out of yesterday's paper?
When I call out for a word, I use gestures:
I fold my hand into a beak, peck at the air,
come up seedless, seedless.

Oh tiny waning fingernail moon, can you tell me
does looking at a faraway thing
bring us any closer to what has slipped away?

Whose child is really mine to mourn?
Raucous clouds of crows darken the skyline,
take to the trees to deliver the nightly news.
How many to a branch until they trip the sour word
you cannot bring yourself to utter?

What Counts as Nearness

1. While physicists and mathematicians
trade arguments like a metronome
   do we ever really touch
   this so-called physical world
   or do we Sisyphus endlessly
   in tragic half-distances
you have us draw hearts on our hands,
palm objects for sentience:
stone, apple, acorn.
We build bodies of evidence
we can wear like fingerprints.
We blossom like a bruise,
turn all the puzzle pieces picture side up,
thumb the smooth fragmented images
hoping we live long enough
to see the whole picture.

2. We talk of beautiful math, scan the sagittal plane,
through which all our names for things
fall, landing on the surface
of whatever we make out with our eyes:
puddle, lake, would we call this a pond?
Already a word is a thing that has fallen,
is a way to say holy,
is a way to hold steady
the gaze of all this wanting.
We call them leaves
because they do.

3. If everything is on its way
into something else,
let us love a moment

for what it is:
a tender parentheses
around this one breath.
Here, near the end of the calendar,
the light comes to us in low angles.
You feel the quiet like a pocket
you want to curl up in,
to attend the patient mending
that only happens
in the dark.

Grammar Lesson

You drive past this field every week
back and forth to a life you've been trying to hold onto.
Watch the grass go from green to gold, then hollow stalk
and think about the ground,
how it stretches out to meet the horizon
like a sentence you could diagram:
(bodies above, bodies below).
You say graveyard and hear the word grey,
drive and cry until your mouth tastes like salt and gravel.
If the tongue knows the feel of every possible object
without ever touching it, what's your excuse
for not bearing witness.
behind between among across
You middle-child your way through rooms,
judge distance by the space between collisions,
trace your way back to look for adjectives where there
were none.
Sometimes you just have to say it plain:
I can't bear another broken heart.
I don't want to know what bombs do to bodies.

Tumbleweeds of winter wheat meet in tangled piles,
parenthetical prayer upon prayer. Nothing's inherently
empty;
to call something hollow is to nod to the loss.
We have different words for presence:
I say: *Listen*; You say, *Here.*
By the time we meet, the sun's already at an angle.
We do poet math over breakfast
each half of our bagel a counter-part taste, honey and salt.
We want both and more and more and all
having found each other at the ages we are.

Katherine Ferrier

Outside, the maple's many paper hands
leave their wet silhouettes on the sidewalk
to masquerade as the past: irretrievable, ghosty,
the precise shape of bodies blown away.

Len Germinara

DEI

There are Polaroid pictures
to prove we existed
Sunday dinners
with the family
        Color television

We walked to school
Played in the woods
and fields without supervision
                Went skinny dipping

I remember Doctors
making house calls

Can't say I remember
Diversity

It was a time of
America
Love it or leave it

Said around breakfast tables
and in classrooms

While we sang
This land is your land
Standing at attention
flags flying
        Proud of our history

Equity
an illusion

Like democracy
Peace and Love or
We shall overcome

We never had hope
when it comes to
Inclusion
We weren't part of the plan

Sepia

Gas lit kitchen hallway
Portal to the inner sanctum
Where beans were baked
Saturdays
In clay pots
wood fired stove

Redolent haze of salt pork
and molasses funk
That led us by the nose
to the kitchen table
Surrounded by a cupboard
full of depression glass
Hampton Beach curios
& Postcards
from Nova Scotia

Echoes of every
dinner conversation
All the way up
to the day
The only son
said
he'd enlisted
to defend his country
in Viet Nam

Ditty for Ferlinghetti

My country's misogyny
If there's a god
What do they think of thee
That's why I sigh

Land where first peoples cried
Land became pilgrim's pride
Nothing short of genocide
No   it's not pretty

Common man's naivety
You were never truly free
Just a dream that we had

Adios to the middle class
Free speech a future past
We are all of a lower caste
And free ain't free

Watching plastic gyres grow
Species expire   I know you know
Who really cares

Please don't remain asleep
Please protect this castle keep
Please think before you in anger speak
Why not give it a try

Man   it is lunacy
Continuing with flawed doxology
C'mon let's   get real

I pray we get a clue
Decency somehow   gets us through
push comes to shove   we all know what to do
and
one slim chance   to get it right

Meme

The setting sun
warms the bird feeders
festooning our back yard

101 pigeons
give way
to a Cabal of ravenous crows

So it goes

The sun
not sure of its setting
busts out some Jesus light   in celebration

Makes majestic
the scene before

Me   *me*

Rocking in a chair
on my back deck

One black image
at the entrance
      to the trail
that leads to the river

meandering through
our backyard

illuminated

She's about the same size
as the crows
A jet-black cat
missing her tail

The embodiment of
violence as harsh
as a 30-degree drop
in temperature
overnight

or a stream
feeding wetlands
diverted
to keep the road dry
in

Winter　　　　*winter*

that is surely
on its way

I call her
Foreshadowing
  For now

Something

to consider when your partner skedaddles in the predawn hours… a coffee stain of words on a post-it note left in the silver salver on the end table by the front door … Reading it, transfixed by the obsession with the mundane… Muttering sounds and sputtering spittle, about time, and how this upsets your routine, after all the morning walk is her duty, while … There he sits, obedient and at your beck and call, his leash and a walking stick at his feet saying with puppy dog eyes… Please take the time to walk me cause… I need to "go" cuz.

Roused from bed at 5
Sleeping dog snoring loudly
Wakes up tail wagging

Eileen Hugo

Summer Porch

Rolled bamboo blinds blocked sun
and the neighbor's view.
So hot we brought the dining room
table out for the evening meal
a private oasis touched by slivered breezes.
A glider and rattan rockers lined up
for after supper sitting, while we children
begged to get back outside.
It was summer and we were out
until the shadows appeared
when the streetlights came on.

As The World Turns

Edging our shores
out of sight of the bathers
Eight million metric tons
of plastic and marine waste
forms a river floating in the sea

Greenhouse gases float into the atmosphere
carbon dioxide, methane, nitrous oxide
fossil fuel, human and volcanic aerosols
Global warming a scientific fact
a political football

Eileen Hugo

Homeless

As the tide recedes
mudflats come alive
shallow pools of guppies
flopping under seaweed
crabs claws click click
bubbling trails of snails
sprouts of water
blown out of
clam pockets
low tide   comfort for some
for others waiting
waiting for night
waiting for the turn
of the tide
the line to move
to reach cover

The Old Cellar Hole

In the old cellar hole the granite is dark
a magic place where fireflies play
in the center a tree and the song of a lark

I found this place at the end of a park
on a warm and bright summer day
in the old cellar hole the granite is dark

greens growing below the edge mark
wild white violets and ferns sway
in the center a tree and the song of a lark

near the hole is an old tin ark
the bottom dissolved by rusty decay
in the old cellar hole the granite is dark

the chiseled stairs are strong and stark
down the stairs a place to pray
in the center a tree and the song of a lark

inside amid ferns to a sound I hark
to the song of the lark as he holds sway
in the old cellar hole the granite is dark

Companionship

We hang out.
Like a best friend
the clicker is at my fingertips.
I am privy to lives I would never have known.
There are the housewives from Dallas, New York,
Orange County, Atlanta and those Kardashian sisters.
Not all frivolous there is the news, the ever-breaking news
There are CNN and FOX. Watch them both and get balanced.
Shows on cooking, building, fixer-uppers, sewing and quilting
If you feel cold, watch an African safari. If you are hot,
the North Pole and floating polar bears will cool you down.
Say you are worried about your home being safe
there are commercials for every home safety store in America.
Watch the detective shows they'll show how easily the bad guys are caught.
If you feel sick or mentally unwell, there are doctor shows
emergency room shows and ever helpful Dr Phil.
Sit down join me

Ann Leamon

The Tarot Card was Death

I drew Death. So much for telepathy—
I wanted the Empress,
sceptered, on a throne,
not a damn skeleton on his white horse,
not when my father, at ninety-four, lay
with his broken back in a hospital bed, alone.

But always read the fine print.
Death's not only death—it brings
transformations,
       new beginnings,
            release
                    from old and useless things.

For all its wrenching change
does Death imply we rearrange
our lives, create another way
escape from homes where every day
the dark-blue curtains always hang
and block the air in summertime,
smoke-filled, cluttered, full of dust
a place his wife believes she must
not leave per orders from the government.

Might he eventually consent
to find a cozy place to live,
someplace bright with friends who give
him company, where he can feed
the birds and read and leave
the lawn care, plowing, wood for heat
to someone who'll cook, keep it neat?

Ann Leamon

Could new life still arise from Death?
Can we make more emerge from less?

Dark December (a villanelle)

Dark December, all the world condenses
around its center fleeing from the cold.
All our glories huddle in past tenses.

Night falls early, darkening the fences
that separate the new fields from the old.
In dark December, watch as the world condenses.

Warmth and light—though scarce—become intensive.
In candles' glow, we gather to be told
winter stories, all framed in past tenses.

Soups and spiced wines bolster our defenses,
while sugar cookie dough will soon be rolled.
With heat and rich smells, window glass condenses.

Shorter days remove all our pretenses.
The lack of light requires us to be bold—
our current glories will become past tenses.

Solstice comes, then daylight's growth commences,
as now our good friends' mittened hands we hold.
Dark December, all the world condenses;
We reawaken glories from past tenses.

The Driver

We were safe in his hands, steady at 10 and 2
holding the skinny beige plastic steering wheel
of the 1968 Plymouth Belvedere station
wagon, taken every vacation, ordered direct
from the factory, dark red
with standard everything
and those new seatbelts
for every passenger.

Returning late from my grandparents'
classic white parsonage
in Monadnock's shadow, my parents'
voices wash over me
like the tide. I doze, cradled within
Dad's driving, diving from the dark of
Rt 101 into the glare
and speed of 95, the bruising rush of
high-speed metal cruising
north from Boston, absorbs us,
like a single fish in the
school. At the toll, a kiss
of cold air on my cheek, Dad
speaks briefly, pulls
away, accelerates to the limit, maybe more,
eager for home. We kids sigh,
settle, stirring only as
the car slows for the back streets,
turns in at our house. Sudden silence
surrounds us as we stumble
grumpy, soft, dream-caught,
to nestle in cool sheets.

No accidents until last year
when he drove
into the dealership window,
into the post box,
into the Jersey barrier at the dump,
into the visitors' car,
into his license suspension at 94.
"I'll get it back," he says, from his rehab bed,
his back broken after falling
in the kitchen, falling
in his bedroom, falling
while he pushed the wheelbarrow
up the ramp. "I have to.
I'm the driver of the family."

Ann Leamon

Abbagadassett Stream

Anyone could belong
to the Abbagadasset yacht club. You needed
a boat, even a canoe, and a bottle
of wine for the annual dinner.
Extra points for a cork.

Only a canoe could fit
under the bridge across the stream
by Mr. Pratt's strawberry
fields. He dreamed
of sailing his 20-foot sloop down
that muddy trickle, out
to the islands of Merrymeeting Bay and
into an adventure
of oceans, shedding his life
of strawberries and Christmas trees
like a down coat
on a spring day.

His boat couldn't
fit under that bridge.

In his fields, I picked
berries, warm and red
as a heart, sodden
with juice, and turned them into
jam that sprawled voluptuous
on winter bread. I planned
my journey, packed
my bags, measured
my bridges. One
would always be too low.

I blew it up.

Decades later, I stopped by Mr. Pratt's farm.
His strawberries looked fine.

Katie Liberman

Causeway Beach

I went to the beach to clear my crowded crown
It was cold and clear, devoid of other people
I found a used needle nestled next to some lobstering rope
in a cradle of bladderwrack
The thoughts bubbled back through the brine to the surface
How had the needle arrived, by man or by sea?
It didn't matter, the harm was already complete

Flotsam

The sunlight feels different on my skin
The air feels just a little thin
Something is shifting within and without
I can never quite put my finger on it
But every autumn my life falls apart
And like sea glass the tides smooth it over
Eternal waiting brings rapid change
Caught adrift with the shifting seasons
Flotsam in the wake of summer spiraling out
Solivagant in sonder passing by
Wondering if the world is passing me by

Dark oxygen

In the darkest abyss
profound production
splitting seawater
into its base elements
Alchemically unaided by life
metallic nodules spark life into the seas
in the form of oxygen

A new discovery of
a very old thing
perhaps the origin of life itself--
Perhaps it's not such a great idea to destroy what we don't know
scraping away at the very thing that provided
before plants ever felt the sun's warmth

Katie Liberman

Attention to Detail

You are the person who hikes a mountain to
summit its peak
and I was always the person who stopped to marvel at every little mushroom
and feel every mossy patch on a stump
Follow the ants marching in a line and the sound of birdsong
Discovering endless worlds beneath my feet

Caught in the complexities of plant roots and spider looms
eventually I'd realize that you had no room
in your heart for me
or my meandering curiosity
You said I'd taught you to appreciate the little things like sundews
The winding game trails that lead through the forests or how to spot
where the chipmunks feasted on pine nuts
Dragonflies hovering over us
that used to be big as cars
before the dinosaurs

I've known the deer and they know me--something you can never claim
To understand the barn owl in the eaves
The way the forest moves and breathes
Pushing and pulling tides of the sea
Endless wonder in the life I see
I must stop to take it all in
To catch my breath and renew within
But you just want to conquer and climb
And maybe that's why you left me behind

Radio silence

Simply out of spite I will profit from my pain
Turn all of my grief into gains
Make every word count
For the countless times I've spent writing about you

Make each and every poem burn
Shame and guilt and grief into your skin
Branded by your own deceit
Know that I have kept all the receipts

All the things that you have said
All your promises that are now dead
Your touch's memory still burning in my head
I have half a mind to pick up the phone just to leave you on read

But the aching feeling still lingers in my chest when you don't call
Radio silence I'm told is healthy for this sort of thing
No matter that I'm left with your sapphire ring
Because you hate diamonds--
And who the fuck else would make it into a fish but me?
And who the fuck else would wear it but you?

I would give you my heart just to hear your voice again
But I already did
And you left it lying on the floor
And tried to stomp on it as I was walking out your door

Karyn Lie-Nielsen

Fire

September 1978, Cape Split, Maine

1. Nobody died except for one cat,
found later during the gasp
and sob sorting through charr
and calcinated rubble.
The only touch of quiet left.
Except for the miracle of finding
my children's smoke-stained shoes
in the ash-dust of the bedroom.

Compact little shoes, Mary Jane
buckles and straps, wooly-eared slippers
neatly posed side by side behind
the scorched smoke-smudge door.

Even that miracle of unhurt room hurts
when too loud someone exclaims
What a mercy! The children!
If the fire had come at night!

2. Our first night in the Cape Split cottage
we slept in delicate security,
the pleasant murmur of waves outside the window.
Then morning came sunlit, but September cool.
We laid a fire in the woodstove.

3. Fire. First taste of flame, one match on crumpled paper.
Fire. Fed with kindling, small bites like pablum, to start.
Fire. Takes solids now, thicker wood, heavier bark.
Fire, its appetite sharpened, swallows air, belches.

Fire, hungry-mouthed, growls inside the stack.
Fire! Ravenous hot-breath and roaring from behind the wall.
Fire! Desperate, like a stomach cleaving to bone.
Fire! Strong full muscled long tongue.
Fire! Urgent, licking shelves, tasting books, my Grandmother's clock.

4. Fire! I rush my children outside.
Huddled together like small cold beetles,
what do we say?
Mommy don't cry.
So long, so long holding on.
So long before taking a breath.
So long until *What a mercy!*
The dragon is slain.

5. Through smoke and waste, ruins:
poor crippled table, sad defeated books,
pieces, fragments, soggy keepsakes.
All those tears.

Careful up the blackened stairway
is a room apart, undamaged,
a row of small shoes.

And in the corner,
curled as softly as a fallen silk scarf,
our white and orange tabby cat
on a tuft of carpet
in morning sunlight
nestled peacefully,
asleep
forever.

Karyn Lie-Nielsen

Hope Takes Both Hands
after the ASL sign for "hope"

Hope takes both hands.
Red hands
like love and hate.
Blind hands
like fear and courage.
Nimble-fingered hands
like friends and enemies,
pulling and pushing.
That's two-handed hope.

Hope starts at your forehead
not the chest,
as you might expect.
Though anger does.
I, me, and mine do too.
But these are singular,
Hope takes both hands.

Just remember
when hope comes
to take your hands
it will always be ahead,
up front, leading the way,
like tomorrow
and will
and you.

The Day I Was Born

In midcentury Midwest America
young men left over from the last war
are gearing up for another. My father,
Deaf, unfit for service, waits

in a room lined with hard-armed chairs,
tears open a narrow pack of gum,
reties his shoes and rattles up a newspaper.
Hearing or Deaf, husbands aren't allowed

in the bleached-out overheated space
where my mother labors alone.
Half a decade since the atomic bomb,
she battles hot sheets, longs

for my father's cool hands along the back
of her neck. From time to time a starched cap
appears, measures, straightens, then leaves
closing the door behind her, no wasted

words for those who don't hear: my mother,
unfit for service because she is Deaf.
On the day I was born, after my father goes through
seven packs of gum and my mother emerges

from a mask of ether, the two of them together
take up their posts outside the glass boundary
watching the other survivor
of their own private struggle. I check my senses,

discover I'm sound. Wailing my call,
I cry out but no one hears. A fast learner,
I wave furiously, my flag, then see their smiles.
My company, my people, my family cheers.

Brushing Kate's Hair

My daughter, Kate, has long honey-colored hair.
Kate's hair is thick and heavy.
Around the edges are loose, whispering threads
reaching out new and innocent,
younger than the wise weight
that hangs down her back.

When she was born she hadn't anything
to brag about. Certainly not hair.
She was curious and naked,
bald as the new moon.
My fingers smoothed the down
of her newborn roundness.
Funny nose and no hair.
A daughter with no hair.

But in the night blonde curls came.
Intuitively I stroked, soothing
the bit of silk, twirling those fine threads,
weaving them through the loom of my fingers.
Promise was there.

My own hair is cut short like dried hay.
My mother's is like curled barbed wire.
But my daughter, Kate, has long honey-colored hair.

Mary Jane Martin

In The Beginning

Right from the beginning,
Eve wasn't having any of it.
No man was telling her
what she could and couldn't do.

We've been missing the
whole point of the story
of Adam and Eve.
Women were
smarter and braver
right from the start.

The author of this story
realized his mistake and
ever since has been trying
to convince us that we
are not what we are.

Tell a person a lie long enough
and big enough and you
are eventually believed.

Mary Jane Martin

Coming Winter

Leaning on the rail while a piece of the setting sun
warms my back, I watch the sails head for the docks,
moving in slow motion like reluctant children.

This harbor will soon enough be empty and quiet. But
tonight this harbor is a melody of seagulls, bells, and
ropes slapping poles, a quiet ruckus of rhythm and blues.

Despite the chill, I linger a while longer till the cold
has me turning up my collar. This evening announces coming
winter when the days will become quiet and we will look for
comfort in lit fires and hot chocolate.

I turn for home.

What Was She Waiting For?

She safely stored her good
dishes in the cupboard
waiting for the right
time to use them.

Her jewelry box is full
of trinkets she never wore.

That new dress, that's
not so new now, hung in her closet
never worn while she waited
for the right time to wear it.

The best poem she ever wrote
was left in her memory bank
forgotten by disuse.

What was she waiting for?

When she died, they put
her good dishes out
for her wake. She was
dressed in the dress never
worn, adorned with a necklace
and earrings found in her jewelry box.

Sadly her poem went up in smoke with her.

Each Spring

Each Spring when the lilacs
reach my bedroom window
and fill the room with its perfume,
I am reminded of the time he bought
a bottle of lilac scented perfume for me
and ran its liquid between my breasts
only to later replace it with his own smell
of musk and sweat.

And each Spring,
when I become restless and cannot sleep,
I think this will be the year
I cut those lilac trees down.

Take Any War

The plaque told me that this was the place
where once it was a field littered from battle,
where mothers searched for sons
and sisters for brothers,
where wives looked for their husbands
and virgins for their lovers.

And all these years later
as I look over this verdant field,
I wonder if their lives were in vain.
So much loss of
futures filled with laughter and love,
newborns never to be.

Only to have nothing change.

Dave Morrison

Empty City

Imagine the biggest city you've ever seen,
bustling with activity and commerce,
building and tearing down and building
again.
Now consider it empty.
It's not easy – a city's reason for
existing *is* people.
We were taught that cockroaches would
outlast us all, and rats. In fact, without
heated buildings cockroaches would
be some of the first to go, and without
human garbage, rats would be nearly
decimated by falcons.

My friend just lost his wife, and I
don't know what to say, except that
my heart aches for him.
I imagine that after years of being a
caregiver his life may become simpler –
fewer forms, fewer trips to the hospital
and pharmacy, fewer agonizing
worries.
I suppose one's house becomes less
cluttered – first the hospital bed
goes, then the pill bottles,
medical supplies.

After several freeze/thaw cycles
asphalt and concrete begins to
crack, weeds and wildflowers
take root. Metal begins to

rust, subway tunnels fall in
on themselves and become
river canyons. Coyotes roam
primeval forests that were
once parks.

Maybe my friend will find that
after a while he has free time he
doesn't remember having and
will plant a garden, dust off the
guitar, write a memoir.
Consider a smaller house.
I picture my friend years from
now, sitting on his porch, coffee
gone cold, time-traveling in
his mind to a thousand days
spent together, while gangs of
birds mob the feeders.

In time, what will be left will be
the sturdy stone structures of
an earlier time; train trestles,
libraries, breakwaters. Our
Roman roads.

In the end, Nature takes
everything back. I hope my
friend can find some small
comfort in this.

Summer Morning Rockland

Young Asian woman in hospital scrubs walking an ancient pug –
Chunky guy jogging with concentration –
Woman riding a Stingray bike to work wearing headphones –
Family unloading luggage at a bus stop –
Couple arguing as they power walk –
Jazz guitar on the radio through an open car window –
Sunburned man waiting at a light in a battered pickup –
A bubble of love in my chest expanding from softball to soccer ball,
warm, painful love for everyone and everything, love wrapped in sadness with a bow of gratitude,
Love that leads me once more,
closer to understanding,
almost acceptance,
almost wisdom,
a favorite song comes on the
radio and I am nearly
Raptured.

How Love Works

I'm not going to do
what I want to do, which
is to buy the cat a little
set of matching luggage and
fill it with small bills, give her
a little cowboy hat and a sign
that reads Will Pay For Gas and
put her by the side of the
road, because that's not how
love works.

What I want to do is outfit her
in a little astronaut suit and
tie on a bunch of helium
balloons. Who doesn't want
to fly, who doesn't want a
heroic adventure? I'd be
making her dreams come true
but that's not how love works.

How love works, if you want to
know, is that you sit quietly while
the cat your wife adores works at
destroying a carpet while the muscles
in your neck get as taut as violin strings
and you agree that she's a rascal,
but cute.

Saved by Rankins

I read the news today (oh boy),
the wrong way to start the day,
and I didn't know if I could
bear it, I didn't know if I could
go through one more day with
a tightly clenched fist in my
chest, the hopelessness rising
to my chin, the geyser of bullshit
that is modern life, the ridiculous
flaming shitshow of our own
making, the embarrassing
needless chaos of it all.

Rankins saved me.

The lights were on in the ancient
hardware store and the doors were
open, the woman behind the counter
helpful and kind, they had exactly
what I needed at a fair price, and
the sun was rising as I drove away with
my stuff, off to work, and I felt the
fierce small seed of hope pushing
up through the black dirt.

Annette Naegel

Upwards

Looking into the canopy
alongside the majestic tree
roots hidden below ground
holding it firmly in place
a mycorrhizal network
trading carbon and nutrients
with other trees

I am grounded here as well
at least
temporarily
yet standing side by side

Reaching upward to gain height,
gather light, become strong,
withstand time
Our lives connected
by the soil underfoot,
nourishing us both

Murmurations

Seen then invisible
A cloud of starlings
glide through the air
catching a breeze
responding to some clue
in unison
an uplift and their wings pivot
aligned with the light
rapid transition
twisting and turning in unison

Their destination
unknown to us
purposeful flight
playful, possibly
The illusion they have disappeared
Had I not looked up
I would not have noticed

We share a space in time
a moment together
Connected-when I pay attention

Purposeful, likely
Playful, of course
A flitter of wings
the flitter of my eyelids
All in a moment

A Walk in the Woods

Walking alone in the woods
Noticing the light, the subtle sounds
Seeing the fabric of the forest
and feeling alive.

Am I separate?
Am I truly alone?
Are eyes upon me,
in a place that is otherwise their home?

Hidden by this tree or that rock
up in the tree tops, or in the dark burrows.

No matter,
we share this place
and respectfully I walk through
leaving nothing
out of place
Only my footsteps lightly marked
in the soil.

Annette Naegel

Fields of Green

Like ripples across a pond,
tall grasses sway in the wind
Light catches the hues of tan, yellow and purple
flower heads allowed to bloom atop
Fescue, Timothy, Meadow Foxtail

Amidst the golden sea of grasses,
hints of wildflowers peak through
Daisies, Buttercup, Milkweed

Life is harbored within this world
of vegetation
Insects, bees, birds
Some species specialized to only nest
amidst the cover of tall grasses
Bobolinks, Savannah Sparrows, Eastern Meadowlarks

An ancient landscape yet cultivated by humans
Providing vistas over hills and valleys
Creating a sculpture, a form so inviting
gentle yet persistent
And very much alive
I am at home among the grasses

Final Act

Just before the long season of
brown, grey and possibly white
There is a final act
a burst of red, yellow and orange
set against brilliant blue and green

A chance to breathe in
color, life, brilliance
before the quiet of winter

How perfectly staged
Nature provides a final act
All plants cooperate
in this symphony of color,
displaying their best

Applause, wait, the curtain closes
the performance comes to an end
Another season yet to come

Sarah Oktay

Deadwood

Ripples frame the horse's reflection
Sweating in rivulets
On the sordid streets of Deadwood
Slurp of mud
Clip-clop grooved hoof
The muck made personified
In shades of brown and more brown
Untamed by wheel or boot
Or cavalcades of curses

The dust whispers conspiracies of
A petrichor choir
Promising peaty green
Mulchy sludge
In springtime

Fresh pine scent wafts from
Acres of trees slashed
Hastily slapped together
For capitalistic facades

Gallons of gut rot
Lubricate the squareheads
Loosen the knots
On the bags of placer gold
stream sifted, rafted
Littering the treads of the railroad ties
Awash in calcitrant blood
Loitering in the lofts of the whores
Lining the pockets of the damned

Show me a shark

Throughout much of COVID
I taught 5th graders over Zoom
Staring out from colorful bedrooms
New York City to rural California
They were clutching their stuffed animals
In costumes
And desperate for content
Mask free
We could communicate as well as the distance allowed

I deal in water
That glimmery, slippery
cascade of electron sharing
Polar solvent
Liquid falling out of the clouds
Flowing onto the mountains
Down muddy rivers
Into the ocean

But the kids want me, need me
Pleaded with me
To tell them about sharks
Craving exotic danger and excitement
Even while bobbing in the pandemic ocean
How close are they? How old?
How many? How big?
We'd go through PowerPoints of sharks
Basking sharks, whale sharks,
Goblin sharks, cookie cutter sharks
Misshapen monsters of the deep
Those stories all more interesting
Than the tedium and togetherness
That even endless fidgeting cannot dispel.

Zen Geology

The angle of repose
Gives pyramids the form they long to inhabit
They stay where they are
Sand and rock tumble and stop
Altitude, steepness, and stability
Fashion a template
Where gravity dictates where we belong

Awakening, gray-green-white limestone weathers
Stop motion images
Wind and rain slough the rock
Soft sculpture, pure presence revealed
Pink-veined granite puts up a fight
Resists change
While harbors fill with silt
These mountains wear down, shed skin, evolve
Become still

We are wearing down
Forming the shapes we were meant to fill
The lives we were meant to lead
Colored in, not always in the lines
We age, mellow, character deepens
Blunts insecurities, pettiness, and fear
Faults funnel pressurized lava
Feelings surface and cool

Holes form
Water gyres gouge depressions
File down the sharp edges
Create tidepools, miniature oceans
Cramped living quarters

Starfish and anemones wave
Basking in the soft pull of lunar motion

Pink coral colonies grow
A metropolis of symbiotic creatures
A carnival of souls
Atolls doomed to lie in piles on pink beaches
In thousands of years

Fine black sand blankets the shoreline
Born of cataclysmic explosions
Basalt screaming, hurled from earth to sky
Fetuses wrenched from molten depths.

Lochs protect hidden treasures
Frigid depths, giant sturgeon
Glaciated shape mimics deep hulled boats
Bathtubs filled with peat
Step locks ferry fish and boats
Up and down a liquid staircase
A fifty-foot pyramid of water
A testament to man's desire
To resist their Buddha nature.

Zen Geology #2 - Deposition

In geology the term for the layers of sediment
that pile up
Over millennia
Is stratigraphy
Governed by the laws of superposition
Youngest should be on top
Mile thick slabs of eroded mountains
Transported by rivers and floods
Pour into the oceans
And build up
Just like the history of our lives

New piles on old,
compresses early years
Memories warp, metamorphize
Like the green and gray ooze made of diatoms
Eventually forming clay
Malleable, mutable

That sandstone was formed in college
When facts seemed permeable
Chalk crumbles,
Our childhood is giving up the ephemeral
Plankton lives that made it
Old age is flint
Sedimentary, compacted, ancient
Made of quartz from the skeletons of sponges
Sparking fires for thousands of years

Our friends and family are not depositional
They are bedrock
Granite forged in the fire of DNA and choice
Metamorphically changing our
Sedimentary layers

Anthropocene

Long before Crutzen, Revkin, and Stoermer
popularized the term
"Anthropocene"
You could see the radioactive evidence
In muddy river bottoms and ocean sediments
Clear as day, dark as night
Of the time when nuclear fallout rained from the sky
The era launched by the Manhattan Project's Trinity test
Blasted over the serene white sands
of the New Mexico desert

Scientists argue over the beginning of our influence
From the dawn of early man taming the fields
Through the smoke and soot of the industrial age
To the reign of the Titans
Birthing nuclear bomb tests with ludicrous names like
Starfish, Bluegill, Tightrope, and Checkmate
Our legacy is littering the geosphere

A stack of black ooze, ash, and clay
Cannot hide the staccato remnants of Chernobyl
Nor the smeared faint thumbprint of Three-mile Island
Ironic that these same nuclear gods
May be needed to spare us the Armageddon of climate change

These are just a drop in the ocean
Now we are building the temple of a new era
The Anthropocene
Planted crops displacing rainforest
More plastic than fish in the ocean within a decade
Domesticated animals outnumber the wild

Sarah Oktay

Waves of invasive weeds and European bees
Have elbowed aside natural biodiversity
Still, we are celebrating our total dominance
On the way to the graveyard

Jonathan Potter

My Neighbor Mows

In Spring, before the grass sidles from its stems
And makes its sudden thrust at light,
My widowed neighbor mows his lawn. His blunt figure bent,
His heavy fingers change the plug,
And with one tug he perfumes his yard with oily fog.
He guns the motor twice, boy-like,
As if to impress a date, and smiles,
Though no date's there to hear, And then he treads his lawn,
First pushing the mower delicately, like a baby carriage
Moving not to wake the baby.
The blade beats empty air.
He drops one wheel exactly in the track he made
And comes treading back, down and back,
Firmly now, waking the Spring.
His duty done, he stops and idles the motor down,
Surveys precise parallels wheeled in the greening lawn,
Then jams the throttle forward 'til the engine roars.
When he cuts the sound he tilts his head a bit,
As if listening, in the loud quiet.

X-C SKI

Sonnet

To prep the skis you first pine-tar the base—
That lovely scent beneath the propane torch—
And next add wax: a slipping carapace.
The heated iron will not let it scorch.
So now you head out to the snow-swept land,
Boots set firmly straight, and poles for push—
Soft gliding there, the "tush" of poles in hand.
Just slip by tangled brush, then by a spiky bush.
It's this hushed trip you'll covet all year round,
As through life you'll stumble on the stones
And trip on roots, ears torn by raucous sound,
And plod through time with pain-filled bones,
    It's why a skier's, for a time, so free.
    You'll find it's worth the prep. I guarantee.

PRESENTS

At Christmas, reflect
On piled illusions from childhood:
Forbidden scintillant packages promised
(Between aunts' shirts and socks.)
You were gunfighter! Engineer!
You were chemist, musician, magician!
But the pistol merely
Popped
And the erector-set windmill looked...
Funny
The chemistry set was like school and *wouldn't*
Explode
The horn fragmented under Uncle Fred
And the magic was
Just tricks even your sister knew.
So at Christmas
We learn the most important thing about life
Early.

Jonathan Potter

Spring less Day
Heroic Sestet

The clouds are sheeted over all the land
And block the sun, the warmth, the energy.
All joys of spring are greyed, the hours expand:
Time, grey as clouds, suffused with lethargy.
The scents of grass and flowers all are dulled;
The fluttered songs of birds are now annulled.

Then drizzle starts to coat the budding trees.
It adds a dullish shine to roads and cars.
The birds all vanish, even chickadees.
Damp dusk slides in; forget about the stars.
It's indoor life, which winter traps us in.
So boring! Sweet as saccharin.

The TV weatherman now does his dance
Before the colored map with moving lines.
"More rain and cold!" he says, and gives a prance
To celebrate the shifts in his designs.
(We'll see the warm spring sun someday, of course,
And with a smile, forget this dumb discourse.)

A Farmer's Advice

That apple: red and green and round
The flesh so crisp, the waxy skin–
One bite will make that cracking sound,
And juice spurts past your happy grin.

The core holds bright-brown shiny seeds
Which makes you think of lawn and land
To plant them there, and feed your needs–
Cascades of sound and taste at hand.

A farmer says, "They won't grow true.
The fruits they give are not the ones you want.
You'll get a tree, but need a graft or two.
On seeded trees, the fruit will be a taunt."

"You'll never guess just what you'll get.
It's just like having kids, you know?
And they'll be fine–there's no regret.
But then there's one with special glow."

"Too bad you can't graft kids," he smiled.
"We'd have some right amazing folks.
A perfect deal, a perfect child,
All that, plus all the dirty jokes."

After Robert Frost

Tamara Saltman

The Shortest Month

Sammy's got three tables filled on a Friday night;
the plow has buried the dwarf cherry. Above the brown lilac
two house finches have started their *I was here first / she's mine*
acrobatics, while the cardinal pair, their red still muted, gorge
on the seeds and nuts in the feeder. The lemon tree under
the grow light has four new leaves and approximately 400 aphids,
and last week one fruit harvested itself onto the cold linoleum floor.

I am tired of wearing one pair of boots and the same three wool shirts
over and over again, but dear God they are warm.
On Valentine's
we got oysters from the fridge on the doctor's back porch,
dropped our twenty into the black box,
and drove them home,
the smell of cold fresh salt marsh filling the car.
We ate some raw
and roasted the rest, and later, in bed under the attic roof,
we pulled the blanket high and fell asleep beneath flannel sunflowers.

On Reviewing My Retirement Account

I used to think winning was mostly the score
of years: 87 beats out 67. I was wrong.

Don't misunderstand! I'm not tired (could I ever be?)
of reunions with daffodils in spring, the smell
of woodsmoke as I rake leaves out from under the maple,
the way new snow lingers in perfect cones on the
seedheads of the tall brown grasses.

It's just, well - what's the point
of all the saving and planning and patience
if you never get around to using the time or the money
for anything worth laughing - or crying - about?

Provisions

Climbing through the old pasture
we walk steadily up a hill the glaciers left.
The sumac is brown in the flat November light;
only one red berry hangs on to the wild rose.

We stop to catch our breath,
listen first to the sound of the two-seater plane overhead, practicing
then to the woodpecker feasting
on an infinite supply of emerald ash borers.

From our perch,
the church steeple is all we can see of town,
white and square, gold ball on the tip surprisingly bright.
God provides everything you need says the sign out front.
Also, *The food pantry is open 10-12 on Fridays.*

The Accidental Gift

A gale has come up the bay; salty rain
splatters the windows as the winter sky slowly
so slowly
eases from black to blue-black
to grey. The stove is on; also the coffee.

I stop to watch the evergreens
bend in a gust, then fall back to upright
as the wind drops. Again and again
they lean forward,
needle fingers waving wildly,

then resting
then waving even more eagerly.
The wind chime is somehow still up,
clanging, and in the basement I hear
the sump pump come on. It is a morning

for witches on broomsticks, hurrying home
before full light; dead leaf tornados in the corners
between the fence and the house;
and there - there! in the river birch - a cardinal
in his soggy red shirt, waiting
as the bird bath fills -

Quantum Mechanics

If I understand the theory, the location of each electron
is not so much a place as a probability: the coffee shops
and bars you should check if you're looking for me.

The electrons in each atom are sometimes here,
sometimes there, never in between.
I sat for an hour today examining the idea

that it's not impossible a piece of me will suddenly
appear in a pink cherry blossom, an elephant,
a raincloud, a turtle, a bridge,

or a drop of the Southern Ocean.
The reverse is also true: yesterday
a few electrons were in Paris and Timbuktu,

today in me, no time spent over the water.
My electrons might just as easily go to prison
or Luby's cafeteria - where there is

decidedly less romance and adventure -
and being part of a bridge might well be rather boring,
until it's not, and there you go

dropping into the raging flood.
The physics says we don't control when or where
but what if we could?

Karin Spitfire

Cyclic Blues

One of those days
hard to keep your chin up
Done plenty, worked on poems, art piece
walked, drank tea, consoled a friend

The house is clean, laundry done
plants watered
dinner planned, in the oven
Christmas cards sent

I could use a cuddle
a shoulder to cry on
grammas long gone
the aunties and mother, too

You old long-term couples
do you do this for one another?
Or is that a fantasy too?
Some kisses, skin on skin, the spooning

It wouldn't fix it
old enough to know that
but it sure could
take up some slack

Anniversaries

I.
Some just have static
like mom's birthday and death day
some years they're louder than others
less background noise and inescapable
pretty much all the deaths are like that
but really arising anytime

Gut vibrations, heart flutters
grating in the ears

Some just slam you with unexpected
torrential outburst
you wonder why and then
remember

A few are birdsong
poignant with a dose of sweet

II.
Then there is the mess of childhood days
accumulated terror threat neglect
a few stick out…
but they have been rung out, hung out
to flap in the wind, bake in the sun
these live as dust motes and mold spores in the lungs
in the villi of the gut brain rising like yeast
when there is too much sour
and in the ankles,
ever ready for the gun shot
that says run

Karin Spitfire

Residues hiding
pulsating
with some crazy internal clock that
reminds me
of the sacred fracas won

Meditation on the Chasm

    I.   Where I Don't Go

The black hole, down the tubes
the slide to the bottomless pit
dark echoless, splayed in the void
        Sometimes I circle the rim
        but I have installed speed bumps

No crazy, wild-eyed turbulence, no cutting
or scratching, no sex with exes
        Sometimes I poke my nails into my skin
        leaving slight half moons

Because I already have
        Screamed bloody murder
        yelled white light terror
        hit the red wall of rage
        keened and lain at the nadir

One does not call upon these places
But the possibility of them arises…

        This grief, this loss
        this change is not there
        but here, here

I burst into tears
weep like something is dying
wonder how I will sleep
where the sun and moon will come up
If I will be scared on the ground floor
But that's the thing
        I am my own ground floor
        I've been a lot of places
        I do know how to come back
        But now I know how not to go
        And I don't have to

II.   Ah, but then

There is the
flagrant, yawning gorge
of grief
arriving after
      the foggy brain
          the putting one foot in front of the other
      the acting as if
the cannon ball hole trajected straight thru your gut
hollow now and somehow not bleeding
blank
the space ahead--emptiness of ether
the aching scratching sadness
gonging
the surrender to gone

III.   And

The unexpected find
wonder
when the abyss itself
is cleared, dispelled,
      (see the book for instructions)
that miracle
when it can freely fluctuate between
a crystalline palace of white light
and
the glorious black of a
moonless milky-wayed
night sky.

Poser

A dam the size of Hoover,
> that no longer needs
> to hold back the Colorado,
> cause there is no water

stops the dry heaves of grief
balled into tiny blood clots
in Elizabeth and Gail's lungs,
cancerous tumors in Lindsay, Judith, Sharon

gags with the lack of saliva
bloated stomachs of
yes the starving children
with not even water

muzzles the red spots of AIDS
appearing now mostly in brown
women, the scatter bombs still exploding
in Vietnam, the ones in Ukraine

> while we build tall buildings with bright
> lights where people sit behind computers
> move numbers representing money
> of so few, so few

and the gratitude, writ large
that I was born white in a time
when a woman could get
educated,

Karin Spitfire

escape
abuse, build a safe house
in beautiful Wabanaki territory
with most all she needs

keeps the dam from being blown up.

Is that a good thing?

"Yesterday each one was a sound"

Marie Howe

Yesterday,
the day before their last day
their last yesterday
each was a sound

Those last sounds,
breathing,
maybe a thank you, I love you,
or this is the hard part…goodbye
to the close but not immediate
the whittling down of who hears…

or these
"I can't breathe"
"Don't shoot"
"Why are you following me for?"
the buzzing of planes
gunfire

A sound, alphabet letters once
symbols of sounds with meaning
Aleph-ox, not just A as in Apple or Abraham
that old patriarch sire of what seems like the longest
half sibling brawl in the world
but really what do I know

If I live to be more immobile
I will learn the Ukrainian alphabet
and Passamaquoddy,
learn new sounds
new ways to shape my tongue

Karin Spitfire

But I am afraid
the howling sorrow of death
the horrifying hollering sorrow of
murder and killing
is close to the same in any language

Daphne Lehava Stern

Sweet Annie

It is my way
to live some things
in memory,
like the scent of sweet annie
at the fair, in the air
the light and happy dancers
the couples holding hands
wearing matching jackets
the free-spirits and singers
the stoners and stone cutters
the flowing skirts and walkers
bright colors, bright sky
the moist bottom jeans when
rising from dewy ground
the works, the farms, the animals, the days
oh the days the full days
the night music, the food
the friends…
the joy
Don't ask me to join the crowds
to stand in lines
to try and repeat what cannot be repeated.
Just hang a wreath of sweet annie on my door
and let me
remember.

Lady of the Lake

Two times a week
I was permitted to stay
one hour the first time.
The schoolhouse, transformed
with chairs ringing the room,
slatted, wooden and noisy,
No decorations, just music on vinyl,
like Bill Haley's Rock Around the Clock.

I danced on my father's shoes
to his elegant foxtrot – the only way
I learned to dance.
He was graceful despite
my weight on his toes.
Alfred, minus his cap, twirled me so fast
I fell down, dizzy.
My head would spin
in the bright lights
of the schoolhouse.

Older kids came and went
with smoke on their clothes
and excitement in their eyes.
But everyone came together
as they all lined up
for the magical "Lady of the Lake,"
which I didn't learn until I was
in my teens.

I watched as summer and winter dancers
came together in flurries of flannel
shirts and skirts, flat shoes

the scent of Zimmie's perfume,
creaking floorboards, springing
to pounding of many feet.
There was punch and cookies I think.
The Lady of the Lake, the highlight
of the Schoolhouse dance,
made the old frame building
surely sway and jump,
and dance itself.

the spoils

we brought you peace
and love and right on,
carry on, freedom,
or the wish for it
and endless hope
we brought a war's end,
fight for equality
free love, communal life,
sweet Annie and flowers
flowers everywhere,
militance and power
blacks, women, vets,
everyone a taste of freedom
the hope of it,
the desire of it
long skirts and loose shirts,
altered states,
high, high, high
we brought you love
We will not leave easy
We will not leave quietly
but we will leave you
gently with all we made
with all we wished for
leave you rich
with memory song, dance,
moon and sky.
we don't want to but
we will... leave you

Only Plants…

I don't remember if the sun rose this morning
over the lake, through the trees - I should recall
whether it cast reflections on my wall, making me pause
and watch them fade. Did they?

How can the day begin when someone is gone?
It seems wrong, when the tears in your eyes flow readily
and the mirror-like glass drops on your lap. Did the sun shine?
Really? Did the day begin? I don't recall.

I refuse the night fall, not ready for darkness
over the lake, the hollow place, where dry eyes blink
and wish it was back then…when the sun rose brightly
through the woods, when only plants died.

Sue Dow Thurston

Idiomatic Lesson

There are those,
I'll not name names,
Who cannot leave well enough alone,
Who cannot just let something be,
But turn over every stone,
Check every angle,
Stir the pot,
Poke a stick at it,
Yet answers found are not.
They plod along with hem and haw,
Since inquiring minds just need to know
The key to unlock the door
To all that ebbs and all that flows.
They hope to solve equations,
Inquiring minds just need to know,
The answers to life's riddles,
Line by line and row by row.
Full-understanding just out of reach,
No risk takers here,
They toss the towel in,
Advancing to the rear.

The Cellist

He was no more than seventeen, so green,
The cello chair with golden hair,
Who moved with each flow
Of the cello bow.
Confident and proud,
He wowed the crowd
While he glanced here and there
Aloft in his chair.
This golden son with supple hands, glowing skin,
Accompanied by piano, viola, violin,
Aptly mastered the musical score
With youthful synapses snapping for sure.
Swaying in frame and with soul full of joy,
The cellist seemed more than merely a boy,
Perhaps the embodiment of so much more,
He was truly heavenly, ethereal for sure.
Fingerings so deft, strings singing from bow,
Flowing and swaying, feeling the glow
Of something so grand, beyond a mere show.
He was no more than seventeen, so green,
The cellist, first chair, with shock of golden hair,
Who excelled at his instrument with masterful air.

Sue Dow Thurston

Crevice Cures

There are things that cure the crevices of soul:

Distant, plaintive train whistles
were music to my childhood days,
Calling me to pause at play
to mind-crawl aboard and ride the rails
from town to town.
My sole companion was my hobo pack
filled with all a child would need.
The rhythmic rumbling, the clickity-clack, lulled me
to imagine universes I would never see
while I watched the world wind away.
The whistle holds mystery and more,
never failing to evoke music, which still fills the soul.

Supple, twining cats, much maligned by some,
s t r e t c h from the beginning of life to its end.
Cajoling them to wear bonnets, sit in carriages,
and recline in cardboard houses,
I had ready playmates in my childhood days.
Now, soft comfort on lonely days,
they circle 'round settling in laps,
quite content and self-assured.
Eyes glint in the darkness, eyes with a knowing
of something all their own.
They are purring motors,
which hum assurance that all will be well.
Cats have ways of curling into the crevices of soul.

Shore birds are sermons on the wing.
Their feeding ritual assures that life continues its order:
sunrise and sunset, sun and moon, work and rest.

The great heron lifts and glides across the flats.
Herring gull drops his find to break on rocks below.
Osprey shrieks from above
while tiny shore birds skitter
to and fro below.
The clock is rightly wound
and the Clock Maker holds it in his hand.
Shore birds, sermons on wing, nest in the crevices of soul.

Sue Dow Thurston

Old Thoughts

Sometimes, more often of late,
Our people, those passed,
Come tip-toeing back
Poking their heads around the curtain.
Is it of mystical, celestial origin
Or just my stage of life?

What do they want
Now that I am older?
They appear in fractured dreams,
In the still of the night,
Or times least expected
When all seemed so right with the world.

It is a bane of old age, I say,
This tendency to reflect back,
Back over years, decades, a half century, more.
So much sand has run through the glass.
So little remains from this pouring
Of salt or sand from our moments of life.
It is
Sifted and found wanting,
Wanting answers to questions,
Questions never asked,
Or asked too late-
Too late to learn
Answers that would add flesh to bone,
Color the skin,
Enhance the story.

Harold Van Lonkhuyzen

Hosmer Brook

Sweaty and out of sorts, I rest,
halfway up to the top.
Dim and bright. Hemlocks.
Ferns on the trail overhead
backlit, light-shot: numinous? Virid?
Words seem
inadequate. Cold water
tumbles down, spreads out
across a slab, rolls into
a pool at my feet.
Light flickers at a boulder.
A water strider
pontoons the surface.
Every stone on the bottom is clear.
Transparency.
That gathers at a thin lip
to give itself again
to gravity.

Sophia's First Crush Distracts Her

"Were you two ever soul mates?" our daughter asks,
looking up from *Modern Mathematics*.
"You seem so different." "Well, opposites
attract," her mother says, hard at the task
of mopping. "Attraction climaxed in our wedding,"
I add. "But then it seemed the differences grew,
that we were strangers, that our lives were skew,
lines neither parallel nor intersecting.
Over time we softened, though, edged close,
as though our two trajectories had veered,
aligned, and in another twenty years
might just approach the Soul Mate asymptote,
bent by our toils with and commitments to
intransigent truths, each other, daughter, and you."

High Places

At the edge of a continent, in sight of the ocean,
on top of a mountain, surrounded by grasses,
diminutive oaks, an ever-blowing wind,
I'm eyeing striations where mile-thick ice
once clawed its mark in the rock. Generations
of teenagers' scratchings tattoo the lean-to.
Startlingly close, a vulture coasts by,
and high places—biblical ones—come to mind,
where some deeply engrained desire, eros or death
hiked people up in search of the divine:
I think of Elijah calling down fire,
the slaughter of Baal's 400-odd prophets,
how easy it is to lose one's way. I pray
that I might safely draw closer, but feel only
a withholding; mystery in this beauty,
but no consummation. Nature has been,
I suppose, desacralized. The temple on Mt. Zion,
after all, came to be seen as God's footstool,
his dwelling place on earth. The other high places
were forgotten, abandoned to birds, snow, children,
though they remained, always, places of possibility,
I'd like to imagine.

Francesmary Vigeant

Sun smiles (3 haikus woven together)

For UKRAINE

sunflowers reflect
smiles on your face when you see
fields of gold flowers

sturdy green stems hold
heavy sunflower blossoms
waving in the wind

what are they saying
to all who dwell in this world? ....
P - E - A - C - E

Sssnooow

(written while on watch for a storm)
    (a metamorphosis)

is such a soft sound
can you hear it falling
as it reaches the ground
that stops it
and let's it melt there
or
piles up pure white
flake upon flake
on the un-giving
surface of a hayfield
lighting up the world at
night as it glows
when lit by moonlight
showing shadows
of barns and beasts
adorning this flat white
canvas with their tracks;
and when the wind
wends its way wildly
whirling & willful
like the red shoes
that could not stop
their dancing feet
and suddenly the snow
spits its venomous
virility at your frozen face
as you trudge
legs lifting through
3, 4 five feet of fluff
& finally - you fall

Francesmary Vigeant

in a heap
in the deep
the birds in murmuration above
and the soft snow shrouds
til Spring's thaw
melts all

I live on Eartha

More importantly I live near the sea
Most important I live in the Dawnland
where the sun rises first on this Continent
I am fortunate.   Though
I don't live on the beach or rocks,
when Mariah blows from the East
I am bathed in healing oxygenated air
of saltiness, even inland
where the hill mountains can be seen.
I am cradled by balsam and birch and
maples and other tall trees
that live together side by side and
give out generously of oxygen
and take in carbon
for their own aliment from cars
that speed by on the paved two lane road.
Though the air here is not perfect
It's a far cry from the industrial
air a thousand miles from here
where I used to live.
I have only to breathe from my belly
to reap the benefits of HERE.
It is my medicine and my staple
I promise to treat Eartha
and our waters
well in return.

Dana Wildes

Bells for Aleppo

The bells are ringing for Aleppo
in chapels, all around the world.

In churches, the bells are ringing,
tolling hours, reporting suffering;

sounding aloud funeral processions
for dying men, women, and children

of a Syrian city; a people under siege.
A fortress where all living souls grieve,

and only the dead can take their leave.
Where clanging bells cannot be heard

over falling bombs, screeching shells,
and the din of incessant explosions.

Holy bells will not ring inside Aleppo
until the devil finally lets this city go.

No one can fully tell this tragic story,
but sacred bells tell all symphonically.

Through the globe the bells are ringing.
In choir spaces, angelic bells are singing

the song of all human hearts and souls.
The lyric of common yearning for truth,

a rhymed quest denied in dying Aleppo,

rings out a sad lamentation we all know.

Across earth memorial bells are ringing.
Listen… hear them sighing and singing;

peeling, reeling, ringing, rolling, tolling on.
Bells are clearing the air of all reasons why

only the devil flies in the skies above Aleppo.
The bells remind, God arrives on the 'morrow.

Compassion

Compassion just cannot be compared
To any other form of comprehension...

It is essential to impart a communication
Emotion comports best with compassion

O passion itself can only be felt completely
When compassion is combined with caring

For the heart is at the center of compassion
Where love can commune with inspiration

Distilling unity from disparate community
Transforming love into vital commitment

Gracefulness surpassing all understanding
Transcending any form of combativeness

Compassion proves irreplaceable if missing
An irreducible ingredient of rapprochement

The secret sauce in recipes for commonality
The only bond of love that co-mingles souls

Without compassion, knowledge complicates
And love alone cannot command permanence

With compassion, knowledge informs loving
Making love last longer than eternity passing

Compassion just cannot be compared
To any other form of comprehension...

New England Stonewalls

I never saw
Ice-age glaciers retreating
Grinding the hardscape into
Mountains and valleys sprinkled
With rivers and lakes and ponds

But I have seen
Many thousands of glacial erratics
Littering our landscape like marbles
Abandoned by careless giants at play

And I marvel at homesteaders who
Systematically removed randomness
Creating short and wide stonewalls
Stoutly standing through the seasons
Passed since the valleys were cleared
And the mountainsides were planted

Something there was about such chaos
(Of undivided rocky pastures revealed
Upon the felling of great timber trees)
That called for careful crafting of walls

Yet the cataract of remaining boulders
Could not be bested despite all efforts
Whilst the desired imposition of order
(Like a first sentence in an epic novel)
Was subsumed by a continual grinding
Of nature's evolving, relentless assault
On permanence (implied by the walls)

Dana Wildes

Nothing eternal nor intractable occurred
Rather the walls themselves kept moving
Sheltering small animals, birds, reptiles -
Caking with leaf debris and icy snowfalls
Dormant, yet alive (in their immobility)

Important, and stubbornly stable markers
Of our determination and our frailty alike

River Journey

Join me (just at dawn) on the riverbank
Where the mists are forming and rising
Where the birds are waking and singing
The air is cool and moist in the sunshine
And possibilities inform our sensibilities

Life itself, unknowable, fully surrounds
Come, we will push out gently in canoes
Just to humor our unconscious pathways
Dipping oars, slicing through waterways
Picking passages we have yet to traverse

Had we the savvy of the mountain cats
Or the vision of bald eagles or of hawks
Had we the instincts of wily wolverines
Or the endurance of wolves on the hunt
We might not choose to be on the river

But being on the river is to be like water
Flowing with might that carries any fight
Getting wet with experience, christened
In the mysteries of rapids, and waterfalls
Eyes wide open to swift currents in time

Submersed in nature's inimitable beauty
Our journey assumes a sacred dimension
As the river awakens, we are in harmony
And if we stop to fish, feeling our hunger
We're no different than any other critter

Too soon echoes the dusky cry of a loon
Telling us it is time to find our campsite

Dana Wildes

Pitching tents; gathering wood for a fire;
Pan frying trout; unrolling bags for night
Preparations in drowsiness for our sleep

For the moment, we gaze upon the stars
Exchanging stories and memories for life
We hear the bard's: "who cooks for you"
As crickets, and tree frogs, sound aloud
Bedded down, we journey on in dreams

The Mourning Dove Sings

The mourning dove, she sings all day
A slow, gentle, and rhythmic calling
Emitting from a cavern deep inside her
Sonorous, soft, and quietly full-throated
Bespeaking a profound sorrow befalling
All within earshot of her melodious song

Seductive, breathy, and so breathtaking
She coos like a winged spirit of sadness
A ghostly presence suspended on high
A herald of brokenness holding us up
On currents of thin air, on lacey limbs
Entwined in a sunlit canopy far above

Beautiful dove of death, dove of music
Faded in color yet brightly lit in peace
Her aspect draws no attention visually
Tho her presence presents us a vision
Surrounding us in hymns enchanting
Lifting us on wings that may fly away

But O that voice carries us clean thru
One humdrum life and on to another
Turning the woods of morning sacred
Making of evening a shining cathedral
Touched by sweet sacramental strains
So melancholy as to be exquisitely holy

Alaina Zyhowski

Snowfall

Snowflakes dancing down,
      pirouetting with purpose,
      each on individual tracks of breeze.

Six-sided beauties with
      rival flare
      bravely diving through the air,

Only to land and melt into their
      neighbors, unifying in one
      peaceful, bright mass.

Are humans capable of
      such collaboration
      amidst differences?

Juxtaposition

It was after dusk.
I walked down the road that followed the sea
in the shape of a 'c.'
The tide was low and so was the moon,
its glowing, waxing crescent
a thin, sarcastic smirk.

It was set in the foreground with Hupper Island behind it,
both bodies dressed in the last faint rays of sunset:
orange at the base, layered with yellow, blue,
then deep indigo on top,
beginning the night.

The saltwater below and the blanket of colors
made the dark silhouettes of pine trees pop.
I took it all in, the beauty of
Port Clyde, the town formerly known as Herring Gut.

I tried to ignore it.
I tried to ignore the machine.
It was there the whole time.
I focused on nature as much as I could,
but I was somehow fascinated by it.

The claw
as quietly as possible,
lowering, opening,
then closing over a boulder that slipped sideways out,
opening then closing again,
in its own bright spotlight,

Just like the 25-cent claw game (or now dollar-sixty claw game)
where rarely a human catches a stuffed animal
or an emoji poop pillow.

Alaina Zyhowski

The orange excavator crane
was perched precariously
on almost-the-edge of a cliff,
perhaps trying to stabilize the land with giant rocks
so as not to let it tumble into the sea.
Then perhaps the house behind the cliff won't
fall into the sea. The ocean, of course,
can be quite temperamental,
but not as much
as humans.

The water was serene,
a glass top
on that crisp, clear winter night. The sky
with the sliver of Earth's moon
and the color stack
stretched across the width of the horizon
enchanted me.

I wonder what it would have been like
if the machine wasn't there. Or if it was
still asleep until later, or the next day.

It surprisingly kept quiet, except for the
occasional creaks and clanks of a
giant metal beast.

Stop

Does anyone put their foot on the
        brake pedal anymore?
Have more people been slamming
        into the car
        two vehicles in front of them
        when
        the one without illuminated
        brake lights
        swerves
        around the side?
Why does it feel like everything is
        speeding up?
Does anyone do one thing
        at a time
        anymore?
Does one eat when they are eating?
Is the food tasted and enjoyed?
Is the phone set aside?
Does eye contact still matter?
Or does it take
        too long?

Take your one-minute vacations:
Smell the flowers.
Pet the dog.
Take a deep breath.
Stop.
Be.

Ecological Transformation

The ocean rising up, filling with meltwaters
Of the polar bears' ice.
How would you feel if your house was melting?
Oh the terror–burning, not just melting,
Your eyes fill with water of their own as you
Evacuate.

A Curious Encounter

Tentatively, both
Reach out to greet each other.
Woah! Suction handshake.

Poets' Biographies

Megan Berman is a member of the Rockport Poetry Group and lives in Rockport, ME with her husband and two children. Megan grew up in Maine and appreciates all the inspiration afforded by living on the gorgeous Maine coast. Megan is a mental health counselor and enjoys writing poetry in her spare time.

Charles Brown was born in Montana but has lived in places as diverse as Illinois, Tennessee, New York and France. He spent most of his professional life as a French teacher in high schools in upstate New York until he retired and moved to Owls Head, Maine. He writes poetry as a way of filling in those idle moments we all have occasionally. A few of his poems have been awarded prizes by the Rockland and Topsham libraries and by the Belfast Poetry Festival.

Eleanor Cade Busby (Ellie) lives in Damariscotta and grew up all over New England, a preacher's kid exposed early on to poetry and Shakespeare, she penned her first epic poem at 4. She attended Goddard College, The Rhode Island Conservatory of Music and The School of Life, majoring in everything she could stuff into her head. She writes because there is no choice.

Steve Cartwright is a retired journalist living in Tenants Harbor, where he serves on the town select board, the Tanglewood/Blueberry Cove Camp's board, and the Millay House board. Passions: Friends, running, swimming, dancing, and music.

Zachary Cole lives and works in Thomaston, splitting his writing time between poems, short stories and novels. He rarely updates his book blog at https://attackthestackreviews.blogspot.com/

Bill Eberle lives in Thomaston Maine with his wife Dagney Ernest and two cats. He has worked at many occupations and avocations including board game design, programming, database and application design, website design and

Poets' Biographies

management, photography, painting, wood sculpting, writing poetry, designing small books and freestyle dancing. Bill began writing poetry more often than occasionally in 2003 and has published a few poems in local newspapers and self-published 10 PDF books of poetry available at BillEberlePoet.com.

Katherine Ferrier is a queer poet, teacher, and multi-disciplinary artist based in Rockland, Maine. Her spontaneous typewriter poetry practice has been featured twice in *The Knot*, and her writing has been featured in *Uppercase Magazine*, *Contact Quarterly*, and several poetry anthologies, including *A Dangerous New World: Maine Voices on the Climate Crisis*, published by Littoral Books, and a self-published collection of photographs and poems about making, called *Thread Says Stay*. She was the Poet-in-Residence at The Press Hotel from 2018-2021, writing custom poems on the spot for guests on one of her vintage typewriters. She has become a regular feature in the arts, non-profit, and humanitarian sectors, writing poems at numerous fundraising and networking events throughout southern and Midcoast Maine. She has recently shown her work at The Ice House Gallery on North Haven, The Buoy Gallery in Kittery, Speedwell Projects and Cove Street Arts in Portland, and the Immersive Media Studio at Bates College in Lewiston. For more information: katherineferrier.net.

Len Germinara lives in Waldoboro, Maine with his wife Sarah Oktay, a dog, and a cat. They moved there in 2023. A Cambridge Poetry Award winner in 2003, he is a former board member of the Sacramento Poetry Center in California and the former Host of "Poets Corner" on WOMR in Provincetown MA. His latest poetry book "Decamerooned" is available on Amazon. His previous book of poetry entitled "Back Story" was released in 2021 and is also available on Amazon. He has been published in various national journals and publications. Len facilitates an on-line workshop for Poetry (Coast to Coast) for the SPC, now in its fourth year.

Eileen Hugo spends her time in Stoneham, MA. And Spruce Head, ME. She's been published in the anthologies of Stoneham's Writers Group *Heels and Souls*, *Southern Breezes*, and *The Baby Boomer Birthright*, published by Poet Works Press, and most recently, *The Taste of Ink*, a collaboration of poets from Midcoast Maine. She serves as a Poetry Editor for *The Houston*

Literary Review. In April of 2015, her book "Not Too Far" was published. In 2018, her poem "Grandfather's Passing" won an Honorable Mention at the Austin International Poetry Festival. Her latest book, "Jenny's Journey", is available now for sale on Amazon.

Ann Leamon has been published in *Tupelo Quarterly, MicroLit Almanac, North Dakota Quarterly*, and *River Teeth*, among other journals. J. Wiley published two editions of her textbook, "Venture Capital, Private Equity, and the Financing of Entrepreneurship". She holds a BA (Honors) in German from Dalhousie University/University of King's College, an MA in Economics from the University of Montana, and an MFA in Poetry from the Bennington Writing Seminars. Ann lives on the coast of Maine with her husband and a corgi-lab mix.

Katie Liberman is a marine educator, writer, and lifelong learner. She's lived for the last eleven years in Maine, from the greater Bangor area, Downeast, Deer Isle, and finally made her return to the Midcoast in 2024. Katie maintains a mini zoo with an elderly cat, a sassy chameleon, hordes of houseplants, and a fish tank on the way. Katie has had a passion for writing from a young age; winning National Novel Writing Month twice, participating in local literary events like Phantom of the Strand, and is currently preparing several novels and poetry collections for publication.

Karyn Lie-Nielsen's poems have previously appeared in *The Comstock Review, Poetry East, Maine* magazine, and broadcast on the MPBN weekly radio program "Poems From Here." Karyn has a chapbook, *Handbuzz and Other Voices*, published in 2015. She is a resident of Waldoboro.

Mary Jane Martin started taking poetry seriously after joining the Moody Mountain Writers, who went on to publish their one and only chat book, "Stone In My Pocket" in 2007. Since then, she's had the privilege of reading her poetry with several awesome local poets. Today she writes with the talented poets of the Thomaston Public Library Poets' Corner.

Dave Morrison's poems have been published in literary magazines and anthologies, and featured on Writer's Almanac, Take Heart, and Poems from Here. Morrison has published

Poets' Biographies

seventeen books of poetry – *We Are Here and It Is Now* (Soul Finger Press 2024) is his most recent collection.

Annette Naegel is a resident of Rockland, has been living on the Midcoast of Maine for the last forty years, soaking in the coast and woodlands of this incredible landscape. Poetry is a brand-new form of expression, presently just being explored. As a novice, she is excited to translate her experience of the natural world into poetry.

Sarah Oktay, PhD, is a chemical oceanographer and the Executive Director of the Herring Gut Coastal Science Center. Her first chapbook, "Sifting Light from the Darkness" came out in 2020. Her second chapbook is coming out in Fall of 2025. She has performed her poetry in person and virtually across the country. She also has published one book of nonfiction, "Naturally Nantucket: The Sea Vol. 1" and has three more coming out, which can be found on Amazon. She has edited eight poetry books. She was the co-host of Spoken Word Nantucket with husband Len Germinara for 12 years.

Jon Potter, who lives in Rockport, has been writing for many years, principally for the theatre, and has published over sixteen plays. He has written two textbooks, one for new English teachers, and one for producers of Commedia dell' Arte comedies, and a novel called "We Will What We Will." He has also published some poetry, in *Maine Stance and Stanza,* (Julie Bragdon, ed.), the *Goose River Anthology* and the *Courier-Gazette.*

Tamara Saltman is a poet-scientist. Her work often explores the natural world and our places in it; she also believes that humor makes everything better. She is a long-time member of Liz Rees' poetry workshop, and her work has been published on the blog of the Sunday Writers' Club. She recently moved to Midcoast Maine from Washington, DC., where she enjoys gardening, singing, making new friends, and exploring the place she now calls home.

Karin Spitfire, a poet and activist conceptual artist, uses whatever medium necessary to get across the message, song, dance, poetry, rant, diatribe, prints, artist books, and letterpress. Spitfire is the author of two poetry collections,

"Standing with Trees" (2006), and "The Body in Late Stage Capitalism" (2021). For a taste, check out karinspitfire.com

Daphne Lehava Stern, is a native New Yorker, and has been here in Maine for the past 47 years. Daphne retired after twenty years on the Hospice Team at Miles. She says "my heart and sensibilities are always with hospice. However, I do find remembering back a learning and loving task!"

Sue Dow Thurston grew up in Rockland, lived briefly in North Carolina and returned to build a home on the Weskeag River in South Thomaston. Between raising three children with her husband, teaching, involvement in various interests and churches, grandchildren and travel, she found time to dabble in writing poetry. She has self-published six books which include two poetry collections and is now working on a third.

Harold Van Lonkhuyzen's work has appeared in the *Journal of the American Medical Association, Christianity and Literature, Christian Century, Spiritus, Eco Theo Review, Café Review, New England Quarterly*, and elsewhere. He's a physician and lives and works in Rockport.

Francesmary Vigeant was born in Chicago, raised and educated in Massachusetts, married with children, and worked in Michigan under the tutelage of Great Lakes. She says "I have found a healing but not easy life getting old, thinking and reading and studying, and writing and performing poetry and living in a haunted creaky leaky house not far from a beloved ocean and near Nature's bounty in the salty state of mystical Maine."

Dana Wildes lives and writes on a mountainside in Rockport, carrying on (shamelessly) with a lifelong avocation. He reads (irregularly) at a few Midcoast poetry groups, to which he (ostensibly) belongs.

Alaina Zyhowski lives in Midcoast Maine Maine. She is a marine and environmental science educator who enjoys telling (and singing and dancing) a story on stage as much as she enjoys writing one.

Thank you

If you'd like to learn more or volunteer for upcoming projects, please visit us at

MidcoastPoetryCalendar.com

Made in the USA
Middletown, DE
03 April 2025

73701483R00095